Bella, the Wildlife Ambassador Series — Book 3

Blue Dives In: Belize's Coral Reefs

By Katie Dolan & Judith Oksner

© Copyright 2020

ISBN 978-1-7339586-4-6

Image credits:

Judith Oksner: Page cover, 1,3,4,5, 10, 11, 12, 15, 18, 24, 33, 35, 40, 43, 45, 47, 48, 49, 53, 54, 55

Susan Scott: Page 11, 16, 17, 19, 21,22, 23, 27, 28, 29, 30, 31,34, 36, 37, 38,

Katie Dolan: Page 8, 9, 26, 32, 39,

Dylan Hattam: Page 6,7

Island Conservation: 51, 52

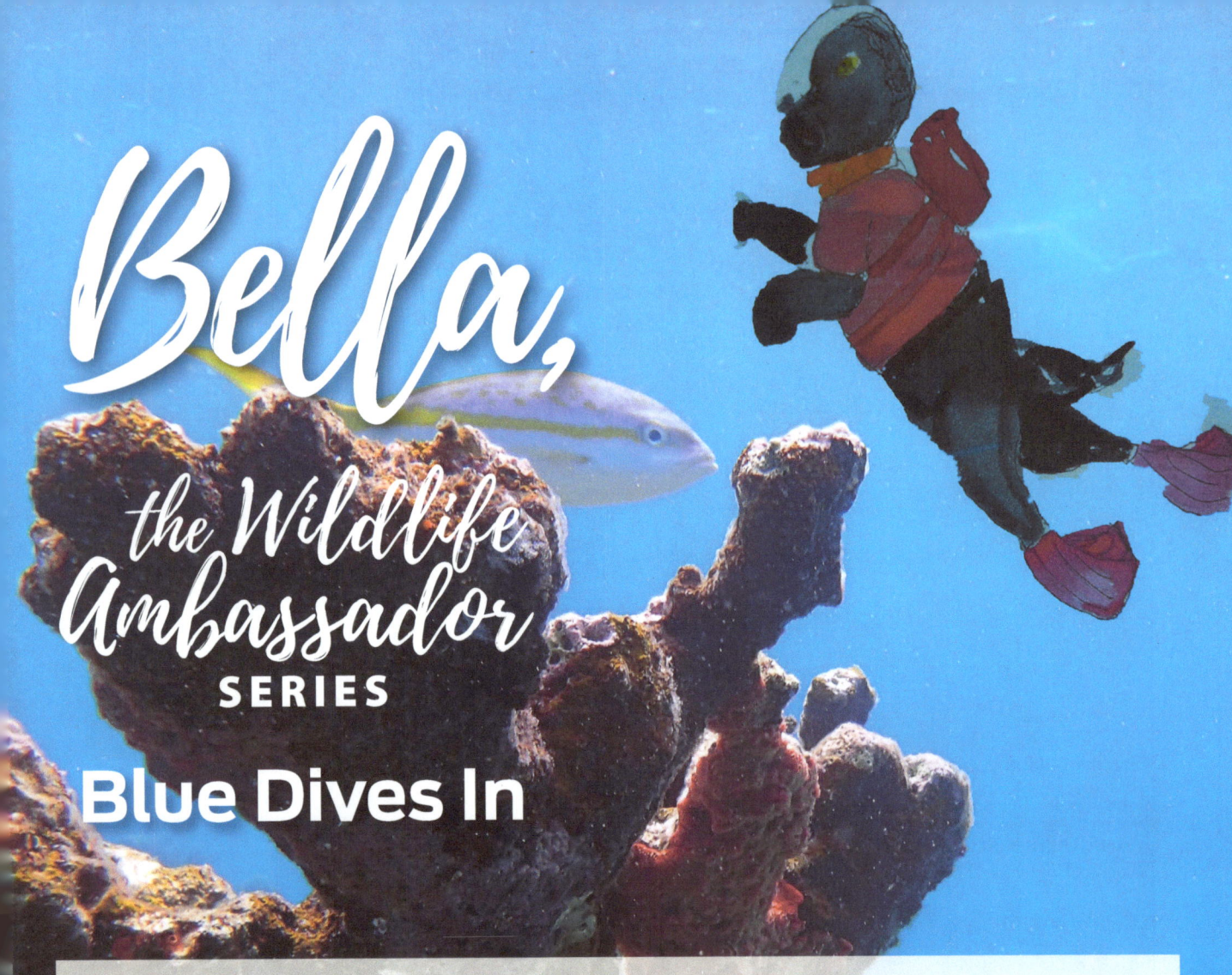

Bella,
the Wildlife Ambassador SERIES

Blue Dives In

The oceans and their smart, adaptive, and beautiful marine animals are in trouble from warming temperatures, changes in water chemistry, coral reef bleaching, overfishing, and pollution. Turn the page to see how Wildlife Ambassadors Bella and Blue help the coral reef residents and seabirds of Belize.

The Wildlife Ambassador series is for families to enjoy together, discovering how we all can help protect wild creatures. Older children will enjoy fascinating facts about wildlife and marine animals as the dogs travel the globe. Parents/grandparents can read the book to younger children while learning ocean ecology from the accompanying sidebars.

Dedicated to the staff of Island Conservation, who work diligently to protect seabirds
and other animal residents of remote islands around the globe,
and to the staff of AZA accredited aquariums,
who educate all of us about our magnificent oceans.

Special thanks for Susan Scott for her
bright fish photos and to Judith Oksner
for her graceful watercolors.

Chapter 1

"*Come on, Blue.* You can do it! Put your muzzle into the water. There's no swell, no seaweed, no jellyfish — it's a perfect day for swimming. Be brave!" I coax my reluctant son to take the plunge. Although Blue enjoys cooling his footpads walking around in the shallows, he's not a good swimmer—yet.

I'm Bella, an older Newfoundland dog and a Wildlife Ambassador for wild creatures. I already know how to swim, snorkel, and scuba dive. I remember when we taught my eight puppies how to swim, using a plastic kiddie pool in the backyard. Several puppies took to the water immediately, while Blue and some of his siblings whined and complained.

Katie's Notes: Newfoundland Rescues

- Gentle Newfoundland dogs are known for cross-species rescues: saving tiny rabbits, squirrels, and, of course, humans.

- A Newfoundland named Hairyman rescued 160 Irish immigrants from a shipwreck in the early 1800s. Swansea Jack also rescued dozens of shipwreck victims. Recently, a ten-month old puppy named Boo saved a drowning man from a river.

- In the early 1900s, the Paris Police added Newfoundland dogs to the force, hoping the dogs would thwart robbers and rescue attempted suicide victims. Unfortunately, the "chiens plongeurs" were inexpertly trained. One dog rescued a ham hock floating down the Seine and devoured it. A thief thwarted his canine pursuers by throwing sausage and bread on the ground.

- Newfoundland dogs were considered necessary rescue equipment in lighthouses along the Atlantic coast.

Now that Blue is grown up, we've accepted a new assignment as wildlife ambassadors for the stressed reef creatures in Belize. Our human, Katie, completed some research on what is happening. She told us warmer ocean temperatures have caused bleaching (unhealthy whitening of the important algae living in the coral colonies). In addition, many marine animals are in trouble due to overfishing and pollution. It will be our first international mission as Wildlife Ambassadors, after we recently helped Piping plovers in Rhode Island and cougars in Colorado.

Blue will need to scuba dive so he can help find out what is happening with the fish and corals. Swimming with his muzzle under water is just the first step on the long road to getting PAWDI (Professional Association of Water Dog Instructors) certified as a doggie scuba diver.

Blue whines nervously, but he finally pushes off the rocks and doggie paddles in circles around the quiet cove. He's splashing, but he'll soon learn to relax and rely on the natural buoyancy of his double coat of fur and the frog kick of his partially webbed back feet. He'll become a swimmer, upholding the proud tradition of Newfoundlands as brave rescue dogs and fishermen's assistants.

"That's it. Looking good, Blue," I say. "Now, try the facemask. We'll want to meet the various reef animals and it will make it easier to talk to them." Blue looks skeptical but he dons a facemask. Our human, Katie, has already told him about a famous certified scuba hound named Mutley.

Blue puts his muzzle in the water and opens his eyes inside the facemask.

"Holy dog," he exclaims, lifting his head out of the water and spitting out his snorkel. "A big brown fish. A starfish! Green seaweed! A lobster!"

Like a fish, he's hooked on the underwater vistas seen with a facemask. It's magical. The ocean covers 70 percent of the globe, but only a handful of land-based species get to enjoy its magnificence. Blue is excited to be an Aquarian Ambassador!

The Magnificent Mutley

- Mutley is a real life golden doodle. His owner built the special gear for his dog and Mutley has done many dive trips.

- Mutley's plexiglass bubble resembles an old-fashioned diving bell. Both the bubble and suit are weighed down so Mutley stays neutrally buoyant underwater.

- After test runs in the backyard pool, Mutley became the world's first and only scuba-certified dog onboard a Caribbean cruise. He even won an Emmy award for a nature show called "Mac and Mutley."

Blue swims around the offshore rocks, getting accustomed to his gear as I act as lifeguard from the rocky shore. His swimming technique has improved, and I watch my son with growing pride. He's a quick learner. He comes out of the water, shaking his whole body and spraying cold Atlantic ocean water all over me and Blue's friend, Dunkin.

"Blue, you did great," says Dunkin, the American Shepherd. Dunkin's humans are Katie's relatives, so he regularly visits us in Rhode Island. He is small and enthusiastic, with more energy than a Newfoundland. He's always bouncing around, trying to play. Sometimes, we are so worn out, we have to tell him to settle down.

"Next, I'll teach you the names of fish and seaweed," I say. "You'll like the cool names for several individuals of a species hanging around together. In the sea, we might see a shiver of sharks, a raft of penguins, or a smack of jellyfish."

"Do you think jellyfish taste good?" Dunkin asks, smacking his lips.

"Yes," I say. "Jellies are considered delicacies in many parts of the world. Maybe we'll all taste jellyfish someday."

Animal Aggregations

A shiver of sharks

A gang of elk

A troop of kangaroos

A romp of otters

A prickle of porcupines

A crash of rhinoceroses

A streak of tigers

A chain of bobolinks

A congregation of plovers

A murmuration of starlings

A rafter of turkeys

A smack of jellyfish

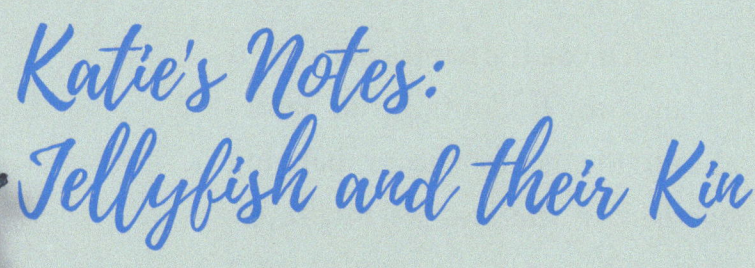

Katie's Notes: Jellyfish and their Kin

The study of jellyfish was very popular during the late 1800s, as Charles Darwin and other naturalists identified many new species.

- Some jellyfish species grow to be as large as a refrigerator; others are tiny. Speaking of refrigerators, jellyfish are considered culinary delicacies in many parts of the world.

- Jellyfish flourish where few other marine creatures venture because they do not need much oxygen. Some jellyfish absorb oxygen into their bells, allowing them to "dive" into anoxic (oxygen-deprived) waters like divers with scuba gear.

- Jellyfish use the same organ to poop and to eat. They release carbon-rich feces and mucus (poo and goo) that feeds carbon dioxide producing bacteria.

- Box jellyfish have sophisticated eyes with retinas, corneas, and lenses. And they have brains, which are capable of learning, memory, and guiding complex behaviors.

- A Portuguese Man-o-war, with its large medusa umbrella and long stinging tentacles, is actually a colony of multiple animals helping each other.

Blue does his course work for SCUBA certification and completes two open water dives in Narragansett Bay with his instructor and class. During the second open water dive, a young female human gets cold (called hypothermia), acts confused, and starts moving in the wrong direction. Blue sees the swimmer's splashes and instinctively moves to rescue her. He swims around the flailing girl and circles back, letting her grab the thick fur around his neck and pulling her back to the boat. Other divers help her back on board and everyone cheers for Blue.

Katie' Notes: Diving Basics

SCUBA Diving was invented in the 1950s. It requires a great deal of gear and planning. Here are a few basic rules:

- When ascending from a dive, come up more slowly than 30 feet per minute. Never travel faster than your slowest exhaled bubbles. Do a safety stop at 15 feet.

- Never hold your breath underwater. As you rise, air expands in your lungs. If you surface too fast, it's possible to cause your lungs to burst.

- Stay hydrated and in shape. Scuba diving is a workout. Make sure to hydrate often, because you are exerting yourself more than you might realize.

- Always dive with a buddy. Remember to let someone besides your dive buddy know where and when you're diving.

- Humans living in communities that free dive (without scuba gear) to collect shellfish have developed eyes that let them see more clearly underwater. In addition, some humans have unusual circulatory systems that keep their core body temperature warm even in freezing waters.

Chapter 2

A few weeks later, Katie, Blue, and I board the plane in Providence, Rhode Island. We are supposed to get VID (Very Important Dog) treatment, as we travel on several different planes to Palencia, Belize. Blue imagines a posh cabin in first class with lots of paw room and steak dinner, but instead we both squeeze into a small space at Katie's feet in front of the bulkhead seats. We point our muzzles up to watch *Finding Newfie*, the in-flight movie on DogTV about a lost seaman's seadog. Then, Katie tells us about oceans and what we can expect to see in Belize.

Katie's Notes:
It's Easy to be Blue
Reading about Our Oceans

- ◄ The term "feeling blue" has nautical origins. If a captain or officer of a ship died while at sea, the crew would fly blue flags and paint a blue band along the ship's hull. Over time, this symbol of grieving was equated with feeling sad or melancholy. Thinking about the ocean's problems can indeed make us feel blue.

- ◄ The oceans absorb ninety-three percent of the excess heat from greenhouse emissions. Increased water temperatures reduce oxygen levels and affect sea life. As the oceans become acidic, marine species — from clams to lobsters — cannot make their protective shells.

- ◄ Thirty-three percent of fish stocks are overexploited. Bycatch (marine animals caught or injured by mistake when fishing for other species) is also a problem. Nearly seventy percent of humpback whales in the Gulf of Maine have scars from being entangled in fishing lines.

◂ Exposure to seawater with large concentrations of carbon dioxide — concentrations projected for the increasingly acidifying ocean — compromises decision-making abilities of reef fish. They swim towards, rather than away from, the predator's scents that they'd normally avoid. They no longer connect predator-related threats with the possibility of an early demise.

◂ Despite these challenges, our oceans can rebound if we take decisive actions: expand marine protected areas, reduce pollution, and leave enough fish in the ocean. Scientists also point to some conservation successes, including rebounding numbers of humpback whales, sea otters, grey whales, and cormorants.

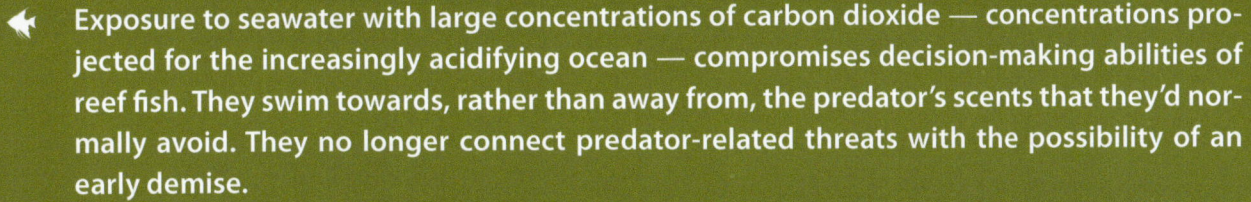

We disembark quietly (no barking!) and jump into a taxi for the short drive into town. Palencia is a relaxed tourist town with a wide boardwalk along a sandy beach: we take a swim in the warm water and rest under the coconut trees. Katie tells us the many ways that humans (and their dogs) depend on the sea, both in the past and now.

Blue's sandy pawprints are gigantic: several kids point to them and approach him. Blue wags his tail, then showers them with slobbery kisses. They jump back and Katie says, "You've been Newfed." She explains that Newfoundlands drool because they have loose lips (called flews) to help them swim in rough conditions without water getting into their mouths. Katie tells us stories about the unique talents and characteristics of the reef animals we'll see, then we fall asleep after the long travel day.

Katie's Notes: Reef Animal Talents

- A cleaner wrasse, a four-inch striped fish, is like a favorite barber, and recognizes individual fish clients who come to its cleaning station. The wrasse remembers where the bigger fish want to be groomed, where their flaky skin is itchy. Cleaner wrasse, like the great apes, bottle-nose dolphins, Eurasian magpies, and Asian elephants, also recognize themselves in a mirror. (The mirror test is widely considered the gold standard for animal intelligence.)

- Many bony fish have an excellent sense of smell. Fish produce an alarm chemical, identified by a German researcher and labelled *schneckstoff*, which translates as "scary stuff." This chemical warns other fish like a fire alarm.

- Pufferfish create elaborate and geometric sand sculpture designs to attract a mate.

- Groupers use body shimmies and head pointing to invite moray eels to hunt cooperatively with them.

- Cuttlefish have depth perception, as if they are permanently wearing movie theater goggles. Scientists figured this out by gluing and velcroing 3-D glasses on the cuttlefish. The hungry cuttlefish detected a mirage of a shrimp, and then were rewarded with a real meal.

- Shoals are gatherings of fish that swim together; schools of fish are more orderly with the individuals all swimming in the same direction.

- Yellow is the most common color for a reef fish.

- Clownfish live within stinging anemone.
  A clownfish protects itself with a coating of slime.

- Parrotfish — named for their big teeth — eat corals and produce up to 10 pounds of sand each day. The sleep at night, often in a familiar rock crevice. The largest males were once females and changed sex as they grew.

Early the next day, we board an open-air boat for the 45-minute ride to the Meso-American reef. It is 65 miles long — the second largest reef system in the world behind Australia's Great Barrier Reef. Blue dons his scuba gear and excitedly plunges into the clear waters. Floating on the surface with his buoyancy compensator inflated, he looks down at the reef.

As I put on my scuba gear, I yell, "Blue, what do you see in the Deep Blue sea?" He barks out key features of the fish species he sees. "Striped seaweed, coral, Ick… Plastic… Why are plastic bags floating here?"

I yell, "We'll discuss ocean plastics after we finish our dive. First, let's meet the reef creatures."

I jump in and start investigating. A school of Blue Tang swims in a tight formation over the reef; yellow French grunts hide under a reef ledge, watching us with large black eyes. A silvery barracuda hovers a few feet below the surface, staring at us with big eyes. A Bahamian Unicorn fish, also known as a filefish, changes color — from white to olive-brown, to grey with bright blue spots. The dorsal spine behind its eyes makes the fish look like a unicorn.

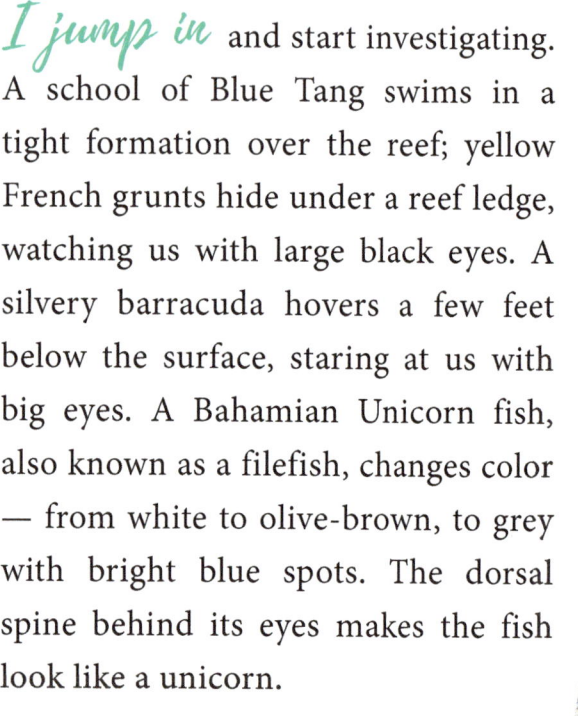

Katie's Notes: Coral Reefs

- Coral reefs support over a quarter of all marine life at some point during the creatures' life cycles. Coral reefs and their fish citizens are in trouble. Staghorn, elkhorn, and other corals have declined by as much as ninety-seven percent in the Caribbean region.

- Careless divers and snorkelers can damage coral with their fins. Coral grow rather slowly, so a broken piece may take many years to be repaired.

- Sunscreen also damages coral reefs. The chemical oxybenzone has toxic effects on young coral, causes DNA damage, and exacerbates bleaching. Around 5,000 tons of sunscreen enters coral reef areas around the world each year, according to the U.S. National Park Service.

- Fish play an important role in keeping coral clean. When researchers played the sounds of healthy vibrant coral reef ecosystems on a dying reef off of Lizard Island in Australia, the total number of fish doubled, and fish species increased by 50 percent compared to equivalent unmodified, silent dead coral.

- Other studies suggest some corals can emit a chemical message which signals fish to come and help clean unwanted algae.

- In reef areas around the globe, special efforts are being made to replant coral reefs: volunteers scuba dive and tie baby coral bouquets of nursery-grown coral to metal structures in Dry Tortuga National Park to replenish the reefs.

I swim up within a flipper's length of a turtle who says, "Hello, Bear. Are you a polar bear that's somehow turned black? And maybe lost?"

" I'm a Newfoundland."

"What's a Newfoundland?" the turtle asks.

I offer a short description of my noble breed: our swimming ability, our courage, and our innate ability to complete ocean rescues.

The turtle listens politely, then says," Maybe you can help some of us, then. My name is Tim. You're just in time for the "Coral Conclave," which some of us have nicknamed "Coral Complaints." Everyone congregates to share worries about the bad things happening to our ocean home. You'll hear all about what is going on… In fact, while I have your undivided attention, let's talk about plastics. Bags and bottles are everywhere; so are the micro (small) bits of plastic floating around. I like to eat jellyfish but can't tell you how many times I've mistaken a plastic bag for a jellyfish. Disgusting."

Katie's Notes: A Plethora of Plastics and Pollutants

- "Flotsam" comes from the word "float," and describes items that weren't deliberately thrown overboard a ship, while "jetsam" (from the word jettison) describes things that were deliberately thrown overboard. There's lots of plastic flotsam and jetsam in today's oceans.

- 10 rivers contribute most of the plastics to the world's oceans. 500 million straws; 2,800 million plastic bags; and 1,440 million water bottles are used once and thrown away every day.

- Every year, about 8 million tons of plastic waste escapes into the oceans from coastal nations. That's the equivalent of setting five garbage bags full of trash on every foot of coastline around the world.

- In developing countries, 80 percent of human waste is untreated and goes directly into rivers and eventually into the oceans.

- There are ways to reduce flotsam and jetsam: an entrepreneur recently created a machine that removes plastics from large swaths of ocean. Japanese scientists have created an inexpensive biodegradable plastic made from starch and cellulose. These technologies, combined with reduced use of plastics and better recycling, can help clean up the oceans.

Tim gestures to us and swims around a tall staghorn colony and into a narrow canyon of coral. We follow him around a bend as the sandy bottom sinks away into darkness. We follow the top of a sloping ridge at a depth of 40 feet and into a natural amphitheater. It's full of marine life: turtles, sharks, reef fish, and parrot fish.

Tim gruffly announces, "Coral Conclave." Blue and I look around, mesmerized by the colors, swaying sea fans and shifting light patterns. We hear a crunching noise as parrotfish eat the coral. A healthy reef is a noisy reef.

A bright French Angelfish leads the coral conclave. He provides a short update on the weather forecast and the number of new lionfish, then says, "The sandy floor is open for new business." A parrotfish stops chewing the coral long enough to complain, "It's too hot in the shallow water. And the branching staghorn corals taste the best, but they are bleaching out faster than the solid corals." A grunt grunts, "And staghorn corals are best for hiding. The brain corals don't offer as many places to get away from predators."

"The noise, the noise of boat engines," a hogfish complains. "It's really terrible." The hogfish looks very grumpy.

A shark swims by in the deep water where the reef disappears into a blue abyss. Blue's bubbles increase: he's scared by the shark and is breathing too fast. I motion to slow

down, hoping he will relax a bit. The shark looks fierce, although Katie's research says sharks are among the most threatened marine species. They are overhunted because people consider shark fin soup a delicacy.

Katie's Notes: Somber Shark Statistics

🦈 25% of shark species are currently listed as endangered, threatened or near threatened by extinction by the International Union for the Conservation of Nature. Sharks are generally slow to reproduce and are disappearing from ocean ecosystems.

🦈 Many shark species are in trouble due to finning, habitat loss, and being caught as bycatch. Generally, only the fins are harvested for shark fin soup, a delicacy in some parts of the world. The still-living shark is cruelly thrown back into the ocean. An estimated 75 million sharks are killed each year for their fins.

🦈 Silky sharks are fierce hunters and like to follow schools of tuna, hoping to enjoy a tuna sandwich for lunch. They get caught as bycatch in tuna fishing nets. When the nets bring up tuna, the silky sharks are often killed by mistake.

🦈 Sharks, as top ocean predators, help keep coral reefs healthy by influencing the mix of fish species. With fewer herbivores, algae become too abundant on coral reefs.

We are nearly out of air and so, after a safety stop at 15 feet below the surface, we slowly rise from the depths and climb back into the boat. What a series of underwater adventures in just one dive! As soon as we get back to land, Katie towels us off with big beach blankets. Getting toweled off is heavenly; I get scratched in all the right places. After Katie notes the morning's highlights in our Dive Logbook, Blue and I settle down for a quick snooze.

Chapter 3

The next day, we return to the same dive spot. Blue swims over to a patch of seagrass and, as his dive buddy, I follow him. "Look: an octopus! Look at those eyes!" Blue says. The octopus, waving a greeting using two of her eight tentacles, says, "Greetings. My name is Pearl. I was watching and listening from my den as you heard the Coral Complaints yesterday. I came out to tell you that things are rough for my kind too. Octopuses are hunted by humans for food since we taste better than a grunt or a hogfish. And, I don't want to brag, but I think we are smarter than your average reef fish. The other creatures down here all do special things, but we octopuses, with highly developed eyes, have a lot of smarts."

"And, you are so beautiful! I can't imagine eating you," Blue gushes.

"Thank you," Pearl says as she turns bright red.

"We will let people know how special you are," Blue promises.

After watching Pearl settle back into her den, Blue swims towards a dark ledge. He stops suddenly. "My dogness! What a stunning fish! I love the stripes and the feathery fins. What is it?" Blue swims closer to the motionless fish to get a better look.

"No, No, be careful," I say. "That's a lionfish. They are terrible, just terrible. There's venom in those spines. Lionfish, who have no natural predators here, eat many kinds of fish, but especially like baby groupers. Now, there are too many lionfish and not enough groupers."

"There's another one! I see five or six just hovering in the coral crevices," Blue says, his eyes darting around.

"Yes, I answer. "They can live in the shallows less than a foot deep and all the way down to 1,000 feet. They can't get rid of them, although scuba divers often come down here and spear as many lionfish as possible. Some ocean locations have over 100 lionfish per acre. I hear humans also eat them, fried like codfish, after they remove the venomous spines."

"We'll have ask Katie about lionfish," I say. "But, first, we should probably talk to more reef fish, okay?"

Katie's Notes: Lionfish

- It is likely that unwanted lionfish were dumped from home aquariums into the Atlantic Ocean. Two kinds of lionfish have been introduced by mistake: one from the Pacific Ocean and one (called the Devil Firefish) from the Red Sea.

- Since lionfish are not native to the Atlantic, they have no predators. They are carnivores that feed on small crustaceans and fish, including young snappers and groupers. Using its long feathery spines, a lionfish traps smaller fish up against the reef.

- Lionfish have venomous spines that can be very painful.

- In an effort to control lionfish numbers, organizations and conservation groups host lionfish derbies with prizes for teams that catch the most lionfish and distribute lionfish recipes.

Suddenly, we hear a deep boom. The reef fish stop moving, like a movie on pause. We look at each other. Many of the fish look fearfully towards the noise, then sprint away. A large creature swims into view from the deeper water.

"It's a young humpback calf," I say between breaths. I enunciate each word.

"Where is its Mom?" Blue replies.

Katie's Notes: Noisy Oceans

- 🔊 At any given time, there are 60,000 commercial ships at sea. That's a lot of noise in an environment where noise can travel very far. In one experiment, researchers played a distinctive sound in the Indian Ocean and detected it in the Atlantic Ocean!

- 🔊 Air gun blasts (used for oil exploration) disrupt marine animal feeding, reproduction, and communications systems. Loud air gun noises actually kill zooplankton, especially krill — which feeds many other marine animals.

- 🔊 Approximately 20,000 fish species are able to hear; at least 800 species make sounds to hunt, mate, navigate or communicate.

- 🔊 A study of stress-related hormones in rare (less than 400 animals) North Atlantic right whales in the Bay of Fundy found that declines in stress level coincided with the temporary decline in global ocean shipping and its noises after the 9/11 terrorist attack.

- 🔊 Solutions to reduce ocean noise from ships include isolating engines from metal hulls, shaping propellers differently, and reducing ship speed.

- 🔊 Loud noise even affects dogs, who can hear sounds four times farther away than their humans. Loud, heavy metal music agitates our canine companions, while soft, classical music settles them down.

We hear another loud boom in the distance. Whales and other marine animals get spooked by seismic air gun blasting used to search for oil deposits. This may affect communications between a mother and her calf and some species may even beach themselves (strand) to escape the chaos. A whale calf cannot survive without its mother's nourishing milk and is vulnerable to predators and other dangers without its mother's protection. Whales, who communicate by sound, may lose track of their families if they cannot hear each other in the vast oceans.

"I'll try to find the mother," Blue exhales.

My son looks at his dive watch and signals that he's got half a tank of air left. I signal back. We'll separate from each other, even though that's not what dive buddies are supposed to do. But it's an emergency and we are here to help. I'll stay with the terrified calf, while Blue looks for its mother. He swims away quickly towards the deeper water and soon disappears into the blue, blue sea.

Katie's Notes: Humpbacks and Other Whales

- Humpbacks are like the Newfoundlands of the sea — they are one of the larger whale species and have been known to rescue seals and people from killer whales.

- Humpbacks swim from cold northern feeding grounds in the Pacific and the Atlantic to warmer waters off Hawaii, Caribbean islands, and Mexico, making the 3,000-mile journey in one month. Groups of humpbacks can herd their prey, creating nets made of air bubble to capture fish.

- Humpback whale songs were documented in the 1950s while the U.S. Navy was listening for Russian submarines. Only the males sing; repeating the song numerous times. They may sing to advertise their presence to females or to sort hierarchical relationships with other males. Songs have similar phrases and themes within each population but vary between populations and change over time. Recordings of these songs have been sent into space in a time capsule and helped expand the "Save the Whale" advocacy movement.

- Unlike most large whales, sperm whales in warm waters usually do not migrate. Carl Safina writes that a sperm whale calf cannot follow its mother to depths of 3,000 feet where she hunts for squid, so aunts look out for and help raise the calf. Sperm whales communicate their whereabouts by loud clicks that can be heard many miles away. Sperm whales use a slapping technique to get little fish to clump together and have even learned to take hooked fish off commercial fisherman's longlines.

- Some orcas have been found to make a speedy 6,000-mile round trip migration — without stopping for food — to warmer tropical waters. They may do this, in part, so they can slough off their skin. Blood must be flowing to shed skin and that doesn't happen in very cold water. In warm tropical seas, however, the flakes fall off and are consumed by gulls and fish.

- Whales also help with nutrient recycling. They forage in deep waters and later their feces float near the surface and act as a fertilizer. Whales also help eliminate carbon from the system. When a whale dies, the very large carcass sinks to the ocean floor, storing a vast amount of carbon.

- Blue whales live 70 years, about as long as Great White sharks. The age of a blue whale can be determined by the pattern of wax in its ears which, like annual tree rings, change from light to dark as the whale fasts during migration or feeds each year.

- Staff at the New York Aquarium have studied whales for many decades. The first Aquarium Director studied 19th -20th century whaling catch logs to assess populations around the globe. In 1966, the same year that humpback whales received international conservation protection, WCS scientists Roger and Katie Payne began a five-year study of humpback whale songs and behavior. And now, Howard Rosenbaum and his WCS colleagues continue this important research, discovering new humpback populations, documenting improved whale numbers in many locations, and studying the impact of threats such as collisions with ships and noisy oceans.

The calf is agitated, making loud distress calls and slapping her flipper against the ocean's surface. I stay quiet, waiting for the young one to calm down.

"I'm sorry the noises scared you. The air guns used for gas exploration are very loud. But, don't worry, my son is looking for your mother. Hopefully, we will find her soon. What is your name?"

"I'm Jack," the calf answers.

"Well, Jack, you sure are big. I am impressed. Everyone says Newfoundlands are large, but I'm tiny next to you. And your mouth opens so very wide."

"Yes, Mom is able to capture many fish or krill in one big gulp," Jack says.

"When you grow older, you'll sing the songs of the humpback whales. That will be a wonderful noise."

"Yes," Jack mumbles. "I usually whisper to my mother, so killer whales don't hear us. And sometimes people on the boats watching us get too close: my mom gets stressed and I don't get to nurse."

I tell Jack about efforts to reduce ocean noises — he'll hopefully grow up in quieter seas. And, since dogs hear better than humans, I definitely understand the discomfort of loud noises such as a T.V. is blaring.

The pressure gauge for my scuba tank shows I'm down to 1,000 PSI (about a third of a tank of air left) and should start back to the boat. Out of the corner of my mask, I see a huge shadow approaching. Jack makes excited, but quiet, noises and swims towards his mother.

With a hurried good-bye, I surface and swim to the boat. I'm hoping Blue will be on board, but it is too quiet. No Blue. We wait for a few hours with the boat anchored, rocking in the gentle swells. It gets late and the sun sets over the sea. The Captain says we must head back to shore. I'm glad the calf and its mother were reunited, but terribly worried we've lost Blue.

Katie and I have a sleepless night worried about my son. We wake early, and I trot down to the town dock. JOY! Blue, like a masthead, is proudly standing on the bow of a boat heading into the harbor! He picks up his gear, jumps off the boat and runs to me, excitedly telling me about his adventure.

Chapter 4

We sit in the shade under a coconut tree as Blue tells us about his adventures.

"I swam out to very deep water and saw a large humpback whale. She was calling for her calf. I said, "Your baby is over there," and pointed towards the reef. The humpback mother quickly swam away. By that time, I was nearly out of air and gradually ascended to the surface. Mom, I even remembered to make a safety stop at a depth of fifteen feet. It was scary floating alone in the blue ocean.

"**When I surfaced,** I couldn't see our boat anywhere. But, I saw an island in the distance, maybe one-third of a mile away. I swam towards the island, remembering that our brave Newfoundland ancestors would swim in the far colder waters of the north Atlantic.

"I finally reached the sandy beach, pulled myself out of the water, took off my scuba gear, and had a long nap. When I awoke, the sun was setting. Hundreds of brown pelicans flew by and divebombed for fish. One of the birds landed on the beach near me. I introduced myself as a Wildlife Ambassador and asked my whereabouts.

"The brown seabird told me her name was Danielle and that I'd landed on Laughing Gull Cay, a beautiful island which is home to brown pelicans, green herons, and melodious blackbirds. Laughing Gulls used to nest on the island too, but the gull colony moved to another island because of all the human noise and commotion. The young pelican explained that her mother was sitting on a nearby nest awaiting the hatching of her eggs."

"Suddenly, we heard a scream from the nesting area. I ran over in time to see a large rat, who ran away when he saw me coming. Danielle's mother thanked me for saving her current clutch of eggs from the nasty rat. I told her we'd encountered problem predators preying on Piping Plovers up north. Another pelican landed near us and regurgitated a small fish at my feet. I thanked the bird for its gift and dutifully ate the raw fish. I had to be a polite ambassador, after all."

"With that, I said goodbye. As I trotted over to the beachfront restaurant to see if I could get a ride back to the mainland, the seabirds screamed and squawked. They were asking me to tell the world about their cousins in trouble because of rats and other invasive species on islands around the globe."

"And to lose the chance to see frigatebirds soaring in circles above the storm, or a file of pelicans winging their way homeward across the crimson afterglow of the sunset, or a myriad terns flashing in the bright light of midday as they hover in a shifting maze above the beach — why, the loss is like the loss of a gallery of the masterpieces of the artists of old time." ~ Theodore Roosevelt

Katie's Notes: Smart Seabirds are Stressed

- Seabirds carefully observe the actions of others in a colony. Guanay Cormorants signal the location of faraway fishing grounds to the birds sitting on nests by flying straight back from the fishing spot and landing in a pattern showing the location of fish. Similarly, Guillemots create an "information halo" which points towards good fishing.

- Over the past six decades, seabird populations dropped by 70 percent. One-third of seabird species are threatened with extinction due to overfishing, human development in nesting areas, climate change, ocean acidification, and invasive species.

- Seabirds which evolved on remote islands without predation by mammals do not have any defenses to protect them from invasive species. In the Pacific, many seabirds are unable to smell a rat, so truly have no ability to protect their nests from predation. Rats and cats are the major threats to the remaining rare wildlife on islands.

- Pollution is a growing threat. Shearwaters can smell the chemical plumes of dimethyl sulphide (DMS) released by schools of krill eating phytoplankton. The birds follow the odor directly to ocean upwellings and fish concentrations. DMS is also released by plastics, which shearwaters mistakenly eat because of the similar smell.

Seabirds are important to island ecosystems because their guano (nutrients) increase the health of coral reefs. Coral near Namena, a seabird colony in the Pacific, had a growth rate four times higher than the coral from another local island with fewer birds.

"*I was very worried about you,* but your adventure let you explore another part of the complicated land-to-ocean web and see how some of the pieces may fit together. Seabirds eat fish, fish eat plankton, plankton like seabird guano, coral reef algae like nitrogen in guano, whales eat krill, and seabirds eat whale skin flakes," I say.

"Yes, and all wild creatures need quiet space away from humans, ships, plastics, rats, cats, and other predators. It's a bit like the Piping plovers: we need to give them room on the remote beaches and make sure there are not too many predators. Those troublesome rats seem to be all over the world. I'd like to help the seabirds, now that I understand their many woes."

I smile, knowing Blue is ready to lead his own adventures as a Wildlife Ambassador. I've taught him well. I may retire and let Blue, with Dunkin's help, lead the next effort.

"We've also been asked to look into diseases which spread between wildlife and pets. We'll start with what is happening to black bears, so we'll be going to the mountains next week," Blue says.

"Well, that's appropriate. We're often mistaken for bears when we're in the woods. I'd like to meet one. I wonder if the bears will be confused by our appearance?" I say.

"And I'm looking forward to working with Dunkin," Blue says.

53

Katie, Bella, and Blue's Suggestions to Help Save Blue Seas

◂ Use reef-safe sunscreen and be careful not to damage corals.

◂ Reduce your use of single use plastics and dispose of them properly.

◂ Participate in a beach clean-up.

◂ Consume seafood responsibly by following the Monterey Aquarium's sustainable seafood suggestions.

◂ Support Island Conservation, the Wildlife Conservation Society, The Nature Conservancy, and other groups working to protect resilient reefs and important ocean habitats for whales and other marine life.

◂ Reduce pollution, including plastics and human waste, wherever water flows to the ocean.

◂ If boating, go slow and look out for whales.

◂ Go to your local aquarium and the New York Aquarium to learn more about the oceans and their inhabitants.

Coral Crossword

ACROSS:
4. Opposite of down
6. Why does the mother humpback leave her calf? (2 words)
7. A moment of quiet
8. A body of water
9. What color are Bella and Blue's air tanks?
11. What kind of diving does Blue learn?
13. A common preposition

DOWN:
1. One of the dog's names.
2. What is the name of the world's first scuba diving dog?
3. Plastic and garbage _____ the oceans.
4. Another word for we?
5. What species of bird does Blue meet?
8. Good, Better, _____?
9. What frightens the brown pelicans?
10. A man-made body of water
12. Abbreviation for the United States

Resources to Learn More:

For Older Readers:

The Human Shore; Seacoasts in History by John Gillis

Becoming Wild by Carl Safina

The Soul of an Octopus by Sy Montgomery

The Dolphin in the Mirror by Diana Reiss

The Breath of a Whale by Leigh Calvez

Why We Swim by Bonnie Tsui

What A Fish Knows by Jonathan Bascombe

Spineless by Jill Berwald

Spying on Whales by Nick Pyenson

For Teachers:

Nature.org on-line learning modules

Island Conservation On-line learning: Seabirds and Invasive Species

National Geographic: www.nationalgeographic.com/environment/oceans/take-action/10-things-you-can-do-to-save-the-ocean/

My Octopus Teacher (Netflix)

For Younger Readers:

The Brilliant Deep: Rebuilding the World's Coral Reefs by Kate Messner and Matthew Forsythe, 2018.

The Secret Life of Fishes by Helen Buttfield, 1999.

What a Waste: Trash, Recycling, and Protecting Our Planet by Jess French

 # Field Notes

www.ingramcontent.com/pod-product-compliance
Lightning Source LLC
LaVergne TN
LVHW070611080526
838200LV00103B/341